Lerner SPORTS

WOMEN'S PROFESSIONAL GOLF

YOLANDA RIDGE

Lerner Publications ◆ Minneapolis

Lerner Publications Company
An imprint of Lerner Publishing Group, Inc.
241 First Avenue North
Minneapolis, MN 55401 USA

For reading levels and more information, look up this title at www.lernerbooks.com.

Main body text set in Aptifer Slab LT Pro.
Typeface provided by Linotype AG.

Editor: Brianna Kaiser **Designer:** Mary Ross **Photo Editor:** Cynthia Zemlicka
Lerner team: Martha Kranes

Library of Congress Cataloging-in-Publication Data

Names: Ridge, Yolanda, 1973– author.
Title: Women's professional golf / Yolanda Ridge.
Description: Minneapolis, MN : Lerner Publications, [2026] | Series: Women got game (Lerner sports) | Includes bibliographical references and index. | Audience: Ages 7–11 | Audience: Grades 2–3 | Summary: "Since the LPGA began in 1950, golf has been full of amazing moments. Discover how the LPGA has grown and learn amazing stats of golfers such as Lorena Ochoa, Kathy Whitworth, and Lydia Ko"— Provided by publisher.
Identifiers: LCCN 2024037516 (print) | LCCN 2024037517 (ebook) | ISBN 9798765668863 (library binding) | ISBN 9798765683613 (paperback) | ISBN 9798765682210 (epub)
Subjects: LCSH: Ladies Professional Golf Association—History—Juvenile literature. | Golf for women—Juvenile literature. | Women golfers—Juvenile literature. | Golf—History—Juvenile literature.
Classification: LCC GV969.L33 R53 2026 (print) | LCC GV969.L33 (ebook) | DDC 796.352/64/0820973—dc23/eng/2024081

LC record available at https://lccn.loc.gov/2024037516
LC ebook record available at https://lccn.loc.gov/2024037517

Manufactured in the United States of America
1-1011722-53857-10/23/2024

TABLE OF CONTENTS

BECOMING NUMBER ONE

On April 21, 2024, Nelly Korda stepped into the tee box. It was the final hole of the Chevron Championship. Korda was leading the major tournament by one stroke. If she finished the tournament with fewer strokes than the other golfers, she would win.

Korda drove the ball off the tee. It sailed down the middle of the fairway. Her second shot landed at the edge of the green. She lined up her shot, but the ball sailed just past the hole. With a second shot, she birdied. She had finished the hole one stroke under par.

Korda held up her fist as the crowd cheered. She had just won the first major tournament of the 2024 Ladies Professional Golf Association (LPGA) Tour. The win was Korda's fifth LPGA title in a row and the 13th win of her career.

FAST FACTS

- IN 1950, 13 GOLFERS STARTED THE LPGA.

- KATHY WHITWORTH WON 88 EVENTS IN HER CAREER—MORE THAN ANY OTHER PRO GOLFER.
- IN JULY 2023, THE LPGA HAD THE HIGHEST NUMBER OF TV VIEWS IN ITS HISTORY.
- IN 2016, 28-YEAR-OLD INBEE PARK BECAME THE YOUNGEST GOLFER TO JOIN THE LPGA HALL OF FAME.

Halfway through the 2024 LPGA Tour, Korda was the highest-ranked player. But holding onto the number one spot is hard. Since joining the LPGA Tour in 2017, Korda had gone up and down in the rankings. Amazing golfers from all around the world compete in the LPGA. And with new and rising talent, golfers always have to be at the top of their game.

Nelly Korda putts during the final round of the 2024 Chevron Championship.

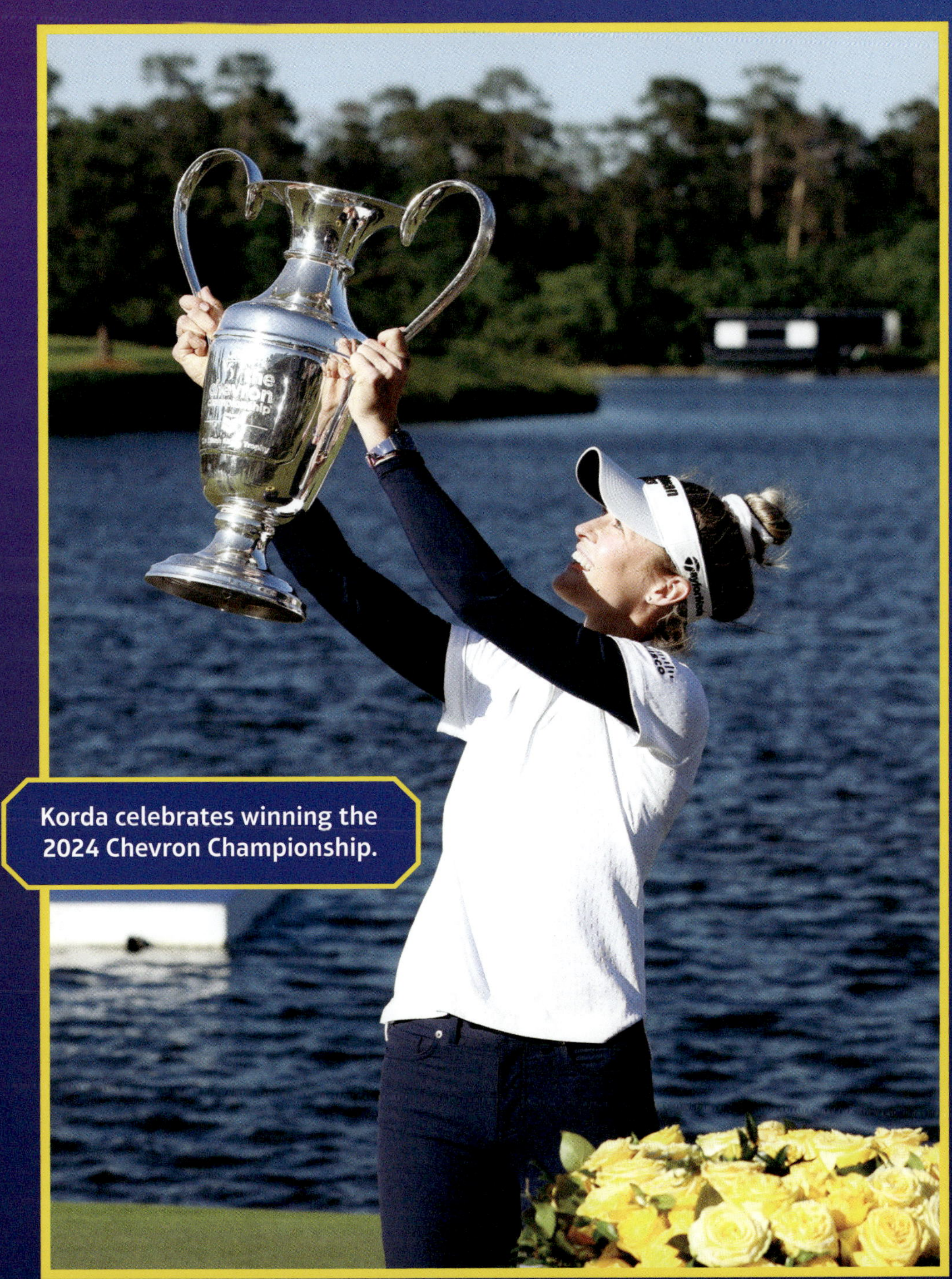

Korda celebrates winning the 2024 Chevron Championship.

Chapter 1

GROWING GOLF

Left to right: The LPGA Hall of Famers Bettye Danoff, Babe Didrikson Zaharias, Louise Suggs, and Patty Berg in 1950

The Women's Professional Golf Association (WPGA) formed in 1944. It was the first pro golf league for women. The WPGA struggled to grow. Fewer than 10 golfers competed in the WPGA in 1947. The league ran out of money and closed in 1949.

In 1950, 13 golfers started the LPGA. This included former members of the WPGA and Hall of Famers Patty Berg, Louise Suggs, Betty Jameson, and Babe Didrikson Zaharias. The LPGA didn't have much money in the beginning. The golfers had to do everything themselves. They even had to set up the golf courses for their events.

Babe Didrikson Zaharias celebrates winning the 1954 US Women's Open.

Althea Gibson golfing in 1953

When the LPGA began, the league only allowed white women to play. That changed in the early 1960s. Tennis champion Althea Gibson became the first Black woman to join the LPGA Tour.

Four years later, Renee Powell became the second Black LPGA player. Powell competed in more than 250 pro tournaments during her career. Her roommate for many of these events was Sandra Post. Post was the first non-American player in the LPGA.

Renee Powell drives the ball at the 1983 Ford Ladies' Classic.

AN LPGA FIRST

Fewer than a dozen Black women have played on the LPGA Tour since it began. Four Black women were on the tour in 2016—the most at once on the tour in LPGA history. They were Mariah Stackhouse, Cheyenne Woods, Sadena Parks, and Ginger Howard.

In the 1970s, the LPGA got a big boost. An American company sponsored multiple tournaments around the world, including a new tournament in California. The Colgate-Dinah Shore Winner's Circle (now the Chevron Championship) became very popular with Hollywood stars. The LPGA started getting more attention. Prize money increased, and more LPGA events were televised.

The LPGA continued to grow. Golfers from all around the world compete in over 30 LPGA tournaments. In 2024, the LPGA had a prize fund of more than $118 million. It was the most in LPGA history.

Annika Sörenstam playing in front of a large crowd in 1995

The biggest LPGA tournaments are called the majors. There used to be four major tournaments. Now there are five: the Chevron Championship, US Women's Open, KPMG Women's PGA Championship, the Amundi Evian Championship, and AIG Women's Open (also known as the Women's British Open). A golfer who wins four of the majors achieves the Grand Slam. A golfer who wins all five majors achieves the Super Grand Slam.

Women's pro golf continues to grow through the LPGA. It set up a teaching group in 1959. Since then, the group has taught pro golfers how to instruct golf.

The LPGA supports programs that introduce more women and girls to the sport. One of the programs is Girls Golf. It brings golf to communities with less access to the sport. It also helps girls between the ages of six and 17 to grow their confidence and build friendships and life skills.

Members of Girls Golf give Minjee Lee flowers after Lee wins the 2022 Cognizant Founders Cup.

RISING STAR

The Epson Tour prepares golfers for a career in the LPGA. Gabby Lemieux joined the Epson Tour in 2018. In 2022, she became the first Native American to play in the US Women's Open.

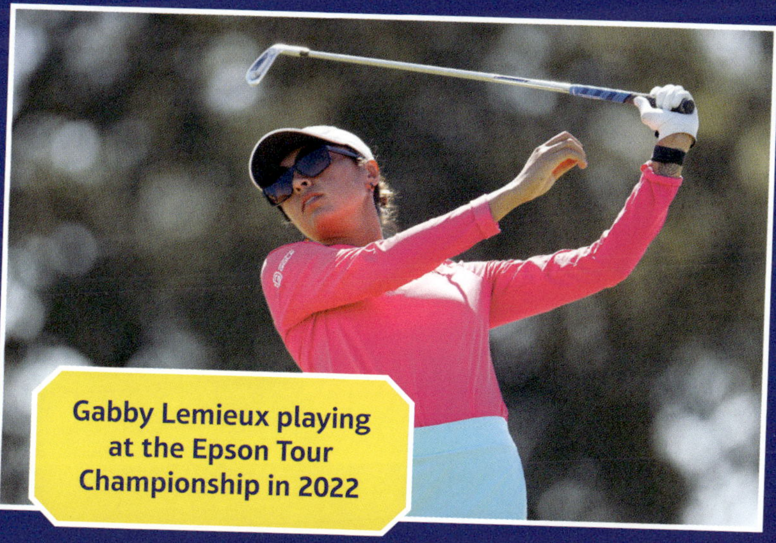

Gabby Lemieux playing at the Epson Tour Championship in 2022

Chapter 2

MAKING HISTORY

Nancy Lopez putts at the 1978 LPGA Championship, now known as the KPMG Women's PGA Championship.

Many great LPGA moments have made history and brought attention to women's pro golf. At the 1978 Bent Tree Classic, no one would have guessed that rookie Nancy Lopez would become part of that history.

Lopez was in the lead until she got bogeys on holes 10 and 11. But on the 17th hole, Lopez scored a birdie. She took back the lead and won the tournament.

Lopez went on to win eight more times in her rookie season. She won the Louise Suggs Rolex Rookie of the Year award and the Rolex Player of the Year award.

Nancy Lopez golfing in 1978

She also won the Vare Trophy—an award given to the golfer with the best scoring average each season. She's the only woman in LPGA history to receive all three awards in the same year.

Kathy Whitworth stood on the green in 1983. She was one shot in the lead at the Women's Kemper Open. Her ball was 40 feet (12 m) away from the hole.

She tapped the ball. It rolled slowly toward the hole. Then it disappeared out of site. Whitworth had done it again!

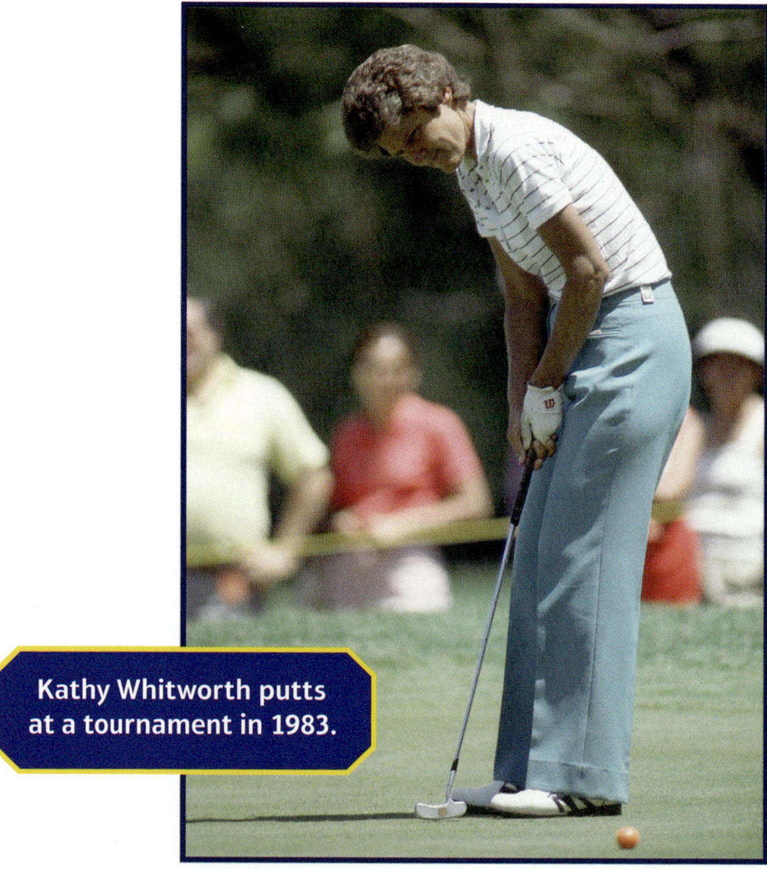

Kathy Whitworth putts at a tournament in 1983.

Whitworth won 88 events in her career. That's more than any pro golfer of any gender. She joined the LPGA Hall of Fame in 1999.

LONG DISTANCES

Laura Davies won 20 times on the LPGA Tour and 45 times on the Ladies European Tour—another pro women's golfing league. From 1992 to 1996, she hit the ball farther than any other golfer. Her longest distance was almost 266 yards (243 m).

Laura Davies putting in 1992

After playing 72 holes at the 1998 US Women's Open, Se Ri Pak and Jenny Chuasiriporn were tied for first place. They played an 18-hole playoff match. But the pair still finished in a tie.

They played an extra hole. Both Pak and Chuasiriporn scored par. Still tied, they teed up again. On the 20th hole, Pak scored a birdie. She'd won at last!

Se Ri Pak celebrates winning the US Women's Open in 1998.

Pak (*left*) and her father, Joon Chul Pak, hold up her trophy after she wins the 1998 US Women's Open.

That year, Pak won another major title and the Louise Suggs Rolex Rookie of the Year award. She finished her career with five major titles and joined the LPGA Hall of Fame in 2007. Her success helped women's golf grow in South Korea.

In 2007, the AIG Women's Open was held at St Andrew's Old Course in Scotland. It was the first time the golf course held a pro women's event.

Allisen Corpuz driving on the 18th hole at the 2023 US Women's Open

Corpuz celebrates her US Women's Open win in 2023.

LPGA Hall of Fame's Lorena Ochoa won the 2007 AIG Women's Open by four strokes. She won seven other tournaments that year, earning more than $4 million. She's the first LPGA player to earn that much money in one season.

In July 2023, the LPGA had the highest number of views in its history. More than 1.5 million people watched the US Women's Open on TV. Allisen Corpuz made par on the 12th hole of the last round to go ahead by two strokes. Fans cheered when she birdied on the 14th and 15th hole, putting her even more in the lead.

The 2023 US Women's Open was Corpuz's first major tournament win. She received $2 million. It was the biggest prize for a single LPGA event.

Chapter 3

BEATING THE BEST

Annika Sörenstam wins a tournament in 2003.

The LPGA is built on great players. Some have been part of the best moments in LPGA history. Others continue to break records and draw new fans to the sport.

Annika Sörenstam rose to the top in the 1990s and 2000s. She had more wins than any other golfer in the 1990s, and she broke or tied 30 different LPGA records in 2001. Two years later, she became one of the few women to ever compete in a Professional Golfers' Association of America (PGA) event. The PGA Tour is a pro golf league in North America that usually only men compete in.

Sörenstam retired from the LPGA Tour in 2008. She ended her career with 72 LPGA Tour wins, 10 major wins, and eight Rolex Player of the Year awards. She joined the LPGA Hall of Fame in 2003.

Sörenstam golfing on a practice range in 2003

Finishing 21 under par, Patty Tavatanakit won Honda LPGA Thailand in 2024. She tapped in a birdie on the final hole to win by one stroke.

Patty Tavatanakit holding up her trophy after winning Honda LPGA Thailand in 2024

In 2015, Inbee Park won the AIG Women's Open. The win gave Park a career Grand Slam. She became the seventh woman to achieve a career Grand Slam.

Park won a gold medal at the 2016 Olympic Games in Rio de Janeiro, Brazil. She had seven major wins and

21 LPGA Tour wins. At 28, she became the youngest golfer to join the LPGA Hall of Fame.

One of Park's competitors at the 2016 Olympic Games was Lydia Ko, who won the silver medal. Ko joined the LPGA in 2014. That year, she became the youngest LPGA player to win both the Louise Suggs Rolex Rookie of the Year and the Rolex Player of the Year awards. At 17, Ko became the youngest golfer of any gender to be ranked number one in the world.

Ko won an Olympic bronze medal at the 2020 Olympic Games in Tokyo, Japan. She also won the Rolex Player of the Year award in 2022. Ko has had two major wins and 20 LPGA Tour wins.

Left to right: **Lydia Ko wins silver, Inbee Park wins gold, and Shanshan Feng wins bronze at the 2016 Olympic Games.**

LPGA HALL OF FAME

Golfers who have competed on the LPGA Tour in 1998 or later must earn 27 points to join the LPGA Hall of Fame. Points are earned by winning LPGA tournaments and Olympic gold medals, or by receiving the Rolex Player of the Year award or the Vare Trophy.

Inbee Park in 2015

Ayaka Furue shined at the 2022 Trust Golf Women's Scottish Open. In the final round, she shot 62, a course record. Furue finished the tournament 21 strokes under par to win her first LPGA title.

With golfers such as Korda, Tavatanakit, and Ko, the LPGA continues to expand. The future of women's golf will be full of new golfers and more exciting moments.

Lydia Ko drives the ball at the 2022 Dana Open.

GLOSSARY

birdie: a score of one stroke under par

bogey: a score of one stroke over par

fairway: an area of short grass between the tee and the green

Grand Slam: winning four different major LPGA tournaments

green: an area of very short grass around the hole where golfers use a golf club called the putter

LPGA Tour: a series of events and tournaments that only qualified golfers can compete in

par: the number of strokes a golfer should take to get the ball into a specific hole

rookie: a first-year player

sponsor: to give money to a sporting event or tournament

stroke: a golf shot

tee box: the area where golfers make their first shot on every hole

LEARN MORE

Abdo, Kenny. *History of Golf*. Minneapolis: Fly!, 2020.

Britannica Kids: Golf
https://kids.britannica.com/students/article/golf/274597

Goldstein, Margaret J. *Meet Nelly Korda*. Minneapolis: Lerner Publications, 2023.

LPGA Hall of Fame
https://www.lpga.com/lpga-hall-of-fame

LPGA-USGA Girls Golf
https://www.girlsgolf.org

Starr, Abbe L. *Annika Sörenstam: LPGA Champion*. Minneapolis: Lerner Publications, 2023.

INDEX

PHOTO ACKNOWLEDGMENTS

Image credits: AP Photo/Gerald Herbert, p. 4; Gregory Shamus/Getty Images, pp. 6, 7, 29; Bettmann/Getty Images, p. 8; PGA of America via Getty Images, p. 9; Ron Burton/Keystone/Hulton Archive/Getty Images, p. 10; Keith Hailey/Popperfoto via Getty Images, p. 11; Robert Beck /Sports Illustrated via, p. 13; Sarah Stier/Getty Images, p. 14; Mike Stobe/Getty Images, p. 15; Leonard Kamsler/Popperfoto via Getty Images, pp. 16, 17; George Tiedemann/Sports Illustrated via Getty Image, p. 18; David Cannon/Allsport/Getty Images, p. 19; Craig Jones/Allsport/Getty Images, pp. 20, 21; Harry How/Getty Images, pp. 22, 23; JIJI PRESS/AFP via Getty Images, p. 24; Andy Lyons/Getty Images, p. 25; Vachira Vachira/NurPhoto via Getty Images, p. 26; Scott Halleran/Getty Images, p. 27; Jan Kruger/Getty Images, p. 28. Design elements: Vect0r0vich/Getty Images; sarayut Thaneerat/Getty Images.

Cover photos: AP Photo/Seth Wenig (Ayaka Furue); Vachira Vachira/NurPhoto via AP (Patty Tavatanakit).